HURRICANES AND TORNADOES

by Richard Worsnop

Introduction

A few years ago a very strong wind blew across parts of Britain. It caused a lot of damage. People were frightened. In some parts of the world strong winds like this happen a lot. In this book you will be able to read about the wind and see what it can do.

Contents

The Great Storm

Look what the wind has done!

It was an October night in Britain in 1987. The wind blew very hard. Sometimes it reached 100 miles per hour. People called the storm a hurricane.

The wind blew a lot of trees down.

The storm did a lot of damage. Trees and cars and buildings were damaged. The police, soldiers and fire fighters had to help people clear away the mess.

Trees fell on to roads and railway lines.

Many trees blocked the roads so people were trapped where they lived. They could not get to work. It took many days to move all the trees.

HURRICANES

This is what a hurricane can do.

Hurricanes begin out at sea. They usually happen in warm countries.

Different countries call these storms by different names. In Japan they are called **typhoons**. In the Indian Ocean they are known as **cyclones** and in the North of Australia people call them **willy – willies**!

Weather forecasters

Weather forecasters are always watching for hurricanes.

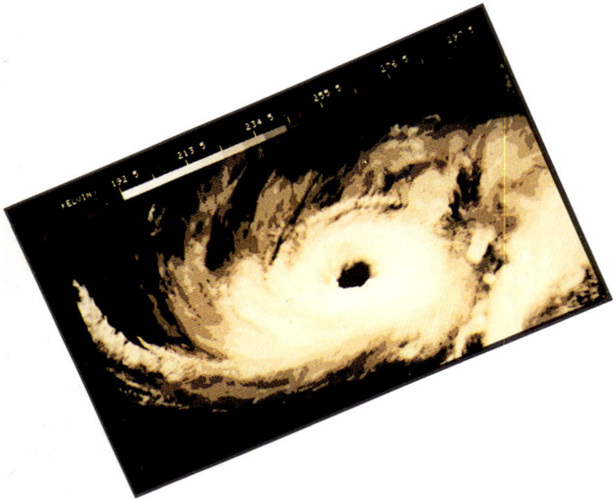

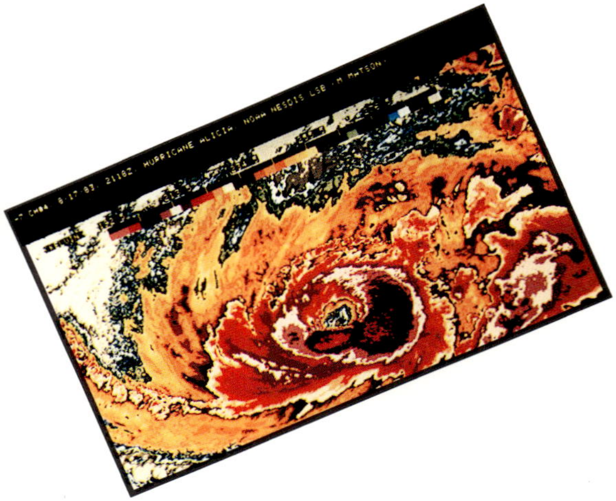

They work out which way the storms are going. They cannot stop a hurricane but they can warn people what is going to happen.

This picture of a hurricane was taken from space. You can see the clouds going round and round.

In the middle of a hurricane

There is no wind at all in the middle of a hurricane!

The middle is called the **eye**. You can see the hurricane's eye in this picture.

TORNADOES

This is the strongest wind. It is a tornado.

The winds in a tornado go round and round at great speed. You can see the wind because it is full of dirt and dust.

Tornadoes can suck things off the ground. Houses, cars and people can be carried away by the wind.

A tornado begins

This tornado is just beginning.

The clouds are getting nearer and nearer to the ground.
All the time they are going round and round in a circle.
The winds are getting stronger and stronger.

A tornado is coming!

Tornado damage

Look what a tornado has done!

The tornado has made a path through the town. A woman was in her kitchen when the winds came. She said later:

"I heard it roar through the chimney and felt it sucking things up. When we stood up there was no roof."

A tornado shelter

This is called a tornado shelter. It is in America. The shelter has been built underground where people can hide from the wind.

Sometimes the wind plays tricks.

Tornadoes suck things up from the ground and then drop them down somewhere else. This aeroplane has been turned upside down.

Dust devils

This kind of wind is called a dust devil. It is a small kind of **whirlwind**.

The wind goes round and round and blows a lot of dust about, especially in the desert.

The Beaufort scale

Wind is measured on the **Beaufort scale.**

The scale starts at 0 when there is no wind.
A strong wind like a hurricane measures 12 on the scale.

3 — 4 — 5

9 — 10 — 11 and 12

The wind can be fun

The wind is not always bad.

It can be helpful too.

Airwell
CLIMATISATION
F.3777
K 990
Airwell

Glossary

Beaufort scale	a way of measuring the speed of wind
cyclone	the Indian name for a very strong wind like a hurricane
eye	the very middle of a hurricane where there is no wind at all
typhoon	a storm like a cyclone or hurricane
whirlwind	a wind going round and round like a small tornado
willy-willy	the Australian name for a hurricane

Index

Acknowledgements

The author and publishers wish to thank the following for permission to reproduce material:

Associated Press **p 8**; The Aviation Picture Library **pp 28 (bottom), 29 (top and bottom), 30 (top)**; Barnabys Picture Library **p 28 (top)**; Crown copyright with permission of Controller of HMSO **p 12 (bottom)**; British Rail/Jeremy de Souza **p 8 (bottom)**; Frank Lane Picture Agency Ltd **cover (left and middle) and pp 13, 15, 16, 17, 18 (×2), 19 (×2), 21, 22, 23, 24, 25**; Gwenan Morgan **p 29 (middle)**; National Trust Photographic Library/Mike Howarth **cover (right) and p 5,** National Trust/Eric Crichton **p 6**; Pickthall Picture Library **p 30 (bottom)**; Glendra Read **pp 3, 9**; Rex Features **p 4**; Science Photo Library/Dan Farber **p 1**; Science Photo Library/NOAA **p 12**; Science Photo Library/NASA **cover (left) and pp 13, 14**; Science Photo Library/Jim Goodwin **p 20**; Gamma Press/FSP **p 10**, G Williams/FSP **p 11**.

Illustration pp 26/7 and design by Patrick Knowles.